UP the sides & DOWN the middle

TRADITIONAL ENGLISH FOLK DANCE

A resource pack for teachers

Eddie Upton and Lyn Paine

Copyright © Folk South West 1996
Copyright © Illustrations Southgate Publishers Ltd

First published 1996 by Southgate Publishers Ltd

SOUTHGATE PUBLISHERS LTD,
15 Barnfield Avenue, Exmouth, Devon EX8 2QE

FOLK SOUTH WEST
The Stables, Montacute House, Montacute,
Somerset TA15 6XP. Tel: 01935 822911

Folk South West works to raise awareness and involvement in the traditional music, song, dance and related customs of the people of the South West. It offers a teacher training course to accompany this pack (See page 48).

Folk South West is a registered charity, no. 1037730.

All rights reserved. Parts of this book may be photocopied and individual tunes copied from the cassette for class work by the purchaser or the purchaser's school/organisation for use within that school/organisation only.

Printed and bound in Great Britain by Short Run Press Ltd, Exeter, Devon.

British Library Cataloguing in Publication Data
A CIP catalogue record for this book is available from the British Library.

ISBN 1-85741-051-3

Acknowledgements

The authors would like to thank: Angela Laycock, teacher at William Barnes County Primary School, Sturminster Newton, Dorset, and David Powell, Headteacher at Burton Bradstock CE VC Primary School, Dorset, for contributing help, support, ideas and material; Lawrence Heath for combining his graphic skills and knowledge of traditional dance to produce the illustrations; Eileen Barrett, Folk South West's administrative assistant, for her fine accordion playing; Paul Burgess for his wonderful musicianship and band tune arrangements; Kim Darby, Chris Lovegrove and the young musicians from Monks Park School and St Bede's School in Bristol for persevering through snow, ice and winter gales to record their music; Ray Williams and Olly Knight of Panda Sound for their infinite care and patience in engineering and editing the cassette; the staff of Folk South West and Dorset Creative and Expressive Arts Team for their help and support; the English Folk Dance and Song Society (supported by the Sports Council) for assistance with the teacher training day at which this pack was piloted; the forty teachers in Dorset for their help in piloting the pack; and the teachers and children of a number of schools in Cornwall, Devon, Dorset, Oxfordshire, Somerset, Tyne and Wear and Yorkshire who have participated in various projects which have all contributed to the process of which this pack is the result.

 Folk South West warmly acknowledges the support of South West Arts towards its work.

Main Cover photograph by Piers Rawson: Children at Culmstock School in the Blackdown Hills, Devon, dancing *The Culmstock Beacon Jig*, a dance they devised during Folk South West's Sights and Sounds of the Blackdowns project in 1995.
Other photos: from other Folk South West schools projects, Bristol and North Dorset Schools Days of Dance, and Burton Bradstock and Avishayes Schools.

CONTENTS

List of Dances in Chapter 5 4
Contents of the Cassette 4

INTRODUCTION 6

Chapter 1
WORKING WITH THE CURRICULUM 7
Dance 7
Music 9
Other Curriculum Links 11
The Whole Curriculum 14

Chapter 2
GETTING STARTED 15
Characteristics of the Music 15
Characteristics of the Dances 18
Partners and Gender Issues 22

Chapter 3
PREPARING YOUR CHILDREN TO DANCE 23
Warming Up 23
Basic Skills 23

Chapter 4
CREATING NEW FOLK DANCES 25

Chapter 5
THE DANCES 27
Notation of eighteen folk dances from across England, from Cornwall to Northumberland, with one dance each from Ireland, Scotland and Wales

GLOSSARY OF TERMS 47

RESOURCES 48

Photo: Piers Rawson

List of Dances in Chapter 5

Dance name	Source
Dorset Ring Dance	Dorset
The Islington Shuffle	New dance
The Cumberland Reel	Cumberland
The Bridge of Athlone	Ireland
Buttered Peas	Yorkshire
Heva	Cornwall
The Snowball	New dance
Up the Sides and Down the Middle	Dorset
The Albert Quadrille	Dorset
The Caerphilly March	Wales
The Barley Reel	Scotland
Three Handed Reel	Devon
Three Meet	Gloucestershire
Goathland Square Eight	Yorkshire
Soldier's Joy	Somerset
Steam-Boat	Devon
Circle Waltz	Northumberland
Bonny Breast Knot	Devon/Somerset

Contents of the Cassette

SIDE B: DANCE TUNES

Tune name	Source
Chelford Races ★	Gloucestershire
Fred Pigeon's ★	Devon
Foxhunter's ★★	Somerset
Coleford Tune ★★★	Gloucestershire
Family Jig ★	Devon
James Higgins' ★	Somerset
Morgan Rattler ★	Dorset
George Till's ★★	Gloucestershire
Bodmin Riding ★	Cornwall
Jenny Jones ★★	Somerset
Morgiana ★	Dorset
The Recovery ★	Dorset

★ Tunes traditional, arranged and played by Eileen Barrett (accordion)

★★ and ★★★ Tunes traditional, arranged Paul Burgess, copyright © Paul Burgess/Folk South West, 1995

★★ Played by St Bede's School Folk Dance Band, Bristol

UP *the sides* & DOWN *the middle*

The order in which the dances appear provides a progression in terms of skills required and elements introduced.

Tune required length and rhythm	Formation
32-bar polka	Circle
32-bar jig	Circle
32-bar jig	4 couple longways
48-bar jig	5 couple longways
32-bar polka	Sicilian circle
32-bar polka	Processional
48-bar jig	5 couple longways
32-bar jig	4–5 couple longways
48-bar polka	Square
32-bar polka	Couple dance
48-bar jig	4 couple longways
32-bar jig	Threesome
32-bar jig	Threesome
32-bar polka	Square
32-bar hornpipe	3 couple longways
32-bar hornpipe	Longways for as many as will
32-bar waltz	Circle
32-bar polka	3 couple longways

SIDE A: TUTORIAL: An introduction to the rhythms and phrasing of traditional folk dance music.

Length and Rhythm	Tape count
32-bar jig	
32-bar polka	
32-bar jig	
32-bar polka	
32-bar jig	
32-bar hornpipe	
48-bar jig	
32-bar hornpipe	
32-bar polka	
32-bar waltz	
48-bar jig	
48-bar polka	

★ ★ ★ Played by Bread Bin, the folk dance band from Monks Park School, Bristol
Additional parts played by Paul Burgess (fiddle, recorder, keyboard) and Eddie Upton (percussion)

Note
You may like to use the last column to mark the counter number on your tape recorder for the beginning of each tune, but remember that the number may vary with different machines.

UP *the sides* & DOWN *the middle*

INTRODUCTION

This pack (consisting of book and cassette) has been devised to help non-specialist teachers work with traditional dance in a fresh, creative and cross-curricular way. It is aimed particularly at Key Stage 2, and is suitable for use from Key Stage 1 to Key Stage 3. It meets National Curriculum requirements for teaching traditional dances of the British Isles, and also shows how work with traditional dance can address other requirements of the curriculum, particularly music.

For many years, traditional British dances (or country dances) have formed part of the school curriculum for some, but not all, pupils in primary schools. Traditional dance has often been delivered as a discrete activity, something quite separate from 'creative', 'expressive' or 'educational' dance. The aim of this pack is to demonstrate how the teaching and learning of traditional dance may be more fully integrated into the dance programme and the wider curriculum.

Britain possesses a wide variety of folk dance traditions. We have not attempted to introduce the teacher to all of them. The focus of this pack is on traditional social dances. These are normally danced with a partner. The notations, however, have been worded so as to render it unnecessary to impose a regime of mixed-gender couples.

The dances have been selected from across England, together with one each from Ireland, Scotland and Wales. Several of the dances have their origins in our home area of the South West of England, but are danced in many other parts of the country.

MUSIC

In order to work effectively with traditional dance, we feel it is important for teachers to acquire a working knowledge of traditional dance music. For this reason, music plays a prominent part in the pack. Side A of the cassette contains a tutorial introducing the rhythms and phrasing of traditional dance music. Side B contains twelve tracks of dance tunes, played in a clearly phrased, rhythmic and danceable style. The tunes are suitable for all the dances in the pack and many more, as well as for the warm-up tasks in Chapter 3.

We hope the pack will help teachers and children alike to discover and develop a highly enjoyable area of curriculum work, and that it may lead to a lifelong affection and enthusiasm for traditional dance.

EDDIE UPTON AND LYN PAINE

Chapter 1
WORKING WITH THE CURRICULUM

This chapter will help you consider the specific curriculum requirements for traditional dance, while demonstrating how the work can have relevance throughout the curriculum.

The Dance Curriculum

In each year of their primary education, all pupils have a dance entitlement. The National Curriculum Programme of Study for Dance states that pupils should:

> perform movements or patterns ... from existing dance traditions (Key Stage 1);
> be taught a number of dance forms ... including some traditional dances of the British Isles (Key Stage 2);
> perform ... set dances, from different traditions from the British Isles (Key Stage 3).

TEACHING STRATEGIES

Traditional dance is a living, breathing, expressive and ever-developing art form, not a dusty relic from the back of the P.E. store cupboard. It is vital, therefore, that teachers employ a range of teaching and learning strategies. This will result in children developing better skills in and knowledge and understanding of dance in general and of traditional dance in particular.

For many years, some of the tensions in education have emanated from the differences between:

- process and product models;
- child-centred and subject-centred learning; or
- open-ended and didactic teaching methods.

For a majority of teachers our own early experiences of school dance comprised the extremes of 'creative' dance (for example, floating like an autumn leaf from a tree) on the one hand and the 'rules and regulations' of 'country' dancing on the other. In this pack we suggest a fresh and more balanced approach to traditional dance, setting it firmly within the dance curriculum, and demonstrating its creative possibilities.

We commend the 'Dance as Art' model (see page 26), in which children develop knowledge, skills and understanding through the interrelated processes of doing (performing), making (planning) and viewing (evaluating), as being just as appropriate

UP *the sides* & DOWN *the middle*

and applicable to traditional dance as it is to all dance forms. The model should help to ensure that all children and young people not only know dances but know how to dance and how to make dances, and learn about dance.

Traditional dance, besides being fun, has a number of features which are important to the teaching of dance generally. These are:

> steps and step patterns
> performance skills
> movement memory
> rhythm and phrasing
> poise, balance, co-ordination
> elevation
> spatial awareness
> formations
> pattern and sequence
> structure
> social skills
> historical context
> local, regional and national context

Many of these also have relevance to other areas of the curriculum (see The Music Curriculum and Other Curriculum Links, pages 9–13).

PLANNING

In order to give all pupils the opportunity to participate in traditional dance, and to achieve breadth and balance of dance activities, as well as continuity and progression, you might wish to consider the following questions.

- How much time per year is allocated to dance?
- How much dance time is allocated to traditional dance?
- Is traditional dance addressed through the curriculum or as an extra-curricular activity?
- Which year groups currently learn traditional dance?
- What facilities, resources and expertise are available?
- What are the aims and objectives of traditional dance sessions?
- What are the school's seasonal requirements?
- Does traditional dance have to be delivered as a 'block'?
- Which National Curriculum requirements can be covered by traditional dance?
- What are the elements of progression in traditional dance?
- How does traditional dance relate to other curriculum areas, topics and themes?

Photo: Simon Chapman

DANCE COMPOSITION

Most of the dances in this pack are traditional because, like folk songs, they were passed on to succeeding generations in family and community by an oral process. In the past, they would not necessarily have been consciously taught by one generation to the next. Rather like community or family folklore, they were acquired or inherited largely by a process of osmosis.

You will see, however, that this pack contains a number of dances devised in recent years. Although these are new dances, they possess similar characteristics to the old ones. We regard the creating of new dances as part of the English folk dance tradition.

We suggest that you encourage children to devise simple patterns of steps and movements in response to music as warm-up tasks (see Chapter 3). Once you have worked through some of the dances in the pack, we recommend that you take this a stage further by leading your children through the process of devising sequences of figures and movements, to create their own folk dances (see Chapter 4).

The Music Curriculum

Music is an integral part of dance. Dancing is truly 'music made visible'. This book and cassette should therefore help you address elements of the Music Curriculum. In particular, use the tape to focus on the musical elements of:

duration,
dynamics,
tempo,
timbre,
texture
and, above all, structure.

Remember that by using the music on the cassette for dance activity, you will be helping your children to:

- listen to and develop an understanding of the music, and to apply this knowledge to their work on traditional dance;
- respond to and evaluate the music, both in performing exercises and dances in this pack and in creating new dances.

The following table (page 10) should help you through this process.

UP *the sides* & DOWN *the middle*

Traditional folk dance music and the Music Curriculum

MUSICAL ELEMENT	KEY STAGE 1	KEY STAGES 2A and 2B
Rhythm – speed, duration and pulse	Respond to a regular beat. Copy, repeat and invent rhythmic patterns. Contrast sound/silence. Hear long and short sounds. Hear faster and slower rhythms and patterns of notes.	Hear groups of beats in twos, threes, fours, etc. (2a). Experience a variety of rhythmic patterns and ostinato (2a). Experience different speeds (2a). Combine rhythm patterns (2b). Experience and understand time signature (2b). Experience off-beat and stressed stressed beats, e.g. hornpipe (2b).
Timbre	Experience different sounds made by a variety of instruments.	Identify sounds made by different families of instruments (2a). Experience different types of sound made in different rhythms (short, crisp notes or longer, flowing ones) (2a). Experience the distinctive sounds made by folk instruments (2b).
Texture	Listen to different sound combinations created by different combinations of instruments.	Experience different sections of music in one tune (2a). Experience accompaniment, e.g. left hand of accordion and in band arrangements (2a).
Dynamics	Experience different volume levels.	Be aware of different volume levels (2a).
Structure	Experience different sections of music. Hear repeated patterns.	Experience musical introductions, phrases, repeats of phrases, melody (2a). Experience melodic sequence and repetition (2b).

Other Curriculum Links

While dance has strong links with Music, you should not forget that it has links with other curriculum areas, such as Humanities, I.T., Maths, History and English. Some of these links are illustrated in the table using *The Snowball* as a model (see pages 12–13).

Teachers and curriculum planners may like to review topics and themes to see where traditional dances could further enhance the curriculum. Some of the dances in this pack, for instance, could link with topics in the following ways:

Pattern and shape	Formations; figures; pathways; use of rhythmic patterns in, say, *Buttered Peas* (page 33), *Barley Reel* (page 39), *The Albert Quadrille* (page 37) and *Three Handed Reel* (page 40)
Structure	The sequence, repetition and structures contained in a selection of dances in this pack
Celebration	*Heva* (processional dance, see page 34), *Bonny Breast Knot* (annual Club Day – see notes with dance, page 46)
Victorians	See notes with *The Albert Quadrille* (page 37). Other dances were very much part of nineteenth-century life in particular parts of the country, e.g. *Goathland Square Eight* in the North Yorkshire Moors, *The Cumberland Reel* in the Lake District.
Change	Progression in dances, e.g. *The Snowball* (page 35), *Circle Waltz* (page 45), *Goathland Square Eight* (page 42), *The Albert Quadrille* (page 37), *Bonny Breast Knot* (page 46)
Local studies	Local/regional dances, e.g. *Dorset Ring Dance* (page 29) and *Up the Sides and Down the Middle* (page 36) for Dorset; *Goathland Square Eight* (page 42) and *Buttered Peas* (page 33) for Yorkshire

UP *the sides &* DOWN *the middle*

The Snowball

A model for cross-curricular work

This table uses the dance *The Snowball* (see page 35) to explore links between a traditional dance and the wider curriculum. Much of the work outlined is based on the idea that the children explore the dance in various ways and then use what they discover to design their own dances. The suggestions are by no means exhaustive, but intended to provide a basis for you to develop your own ideas.

ENGLISH
Writing, Reading, Speaking and Listening

Once the children have become familiar with dancing *The Snowball*, ask them to write down a set of instructions to explain how it is danced. Encourage them to experiment in using, for example, diagrams, symbols, or mathematical language.

Ask the children, working in groups, to make up their own dances. They should notate their dance and then give their instructions to another group who should then try to follow the dance.

Explore the idea of the dance title, *The Snowball*. Help the children to understand the significance of the snowball dance building up layers, just as a snowball gathers snow as it rolls down a snowy hill.

Encourage them to consider using this idea as a framework when devising their own dances.

Children can also try to pass on their ideas orally, effectively becoming 'callers'.

MUSIC

Any dance activity offers opportunities for children to explore music through movement, and vice versa.

To dance *The Snowball* children have to be able to identify musical sequences that define elements of the dance. Use this idea to encourage the children to compose 4, 8, 16 and 32-bar phrases of music to fit the dances they invent.

Consider using computer programs to support this activity.

INFORMATION TECHNOLOGY

Let the children use programmable toys (e.g. Roamer) at Key Stage 1, Levels 1–2 to compose and perform a dance.

Using Logo program, ask the 'turtle' to cast out and back to its starting point. Consider angle, distance, etc.

Use various art and word-processing packages to explore ways of designing and representing dance notation.

ART AND DESIGN

Ask the children to consider the best ways of presenting pictorially the stages of the dance. Encourage them to design a costume that could be worn when dancing *The Snowball.*

HISTORY
Historical enquiry/local history

Encourage the children to find out about social dances in the past.

What dances did elderly relatives or neighbours dance when they were young?

At what special occasions did they dance?

When were special celebrations held: in the family? in the community? at any special times of year (e.g. harvest, Christmas, Shrove Tuesday, May, Whitsun)?

What happened at these celebrations (e.g. bonfire, special food, dressing up, giving presents, processions)?

What musical instruments did local dance musicians play?

GEOGRAPHY

Draw a series of maps of the group 'frozen' at different stages of the dance. Build these into the set of instructions (see English box).

Allow the children to devise their own symbols to represent dancers, direction of movement, etc.

P.E.

Traditional dance is part of the P.E. curriculum. Read the three elements of the Dance Programmes of Study at Key Stages 1 and 2 and see how many can be addressed through the medium of traditional dance.

Consider also the opportunities for peer evaluation of dances and dance sequences.

MATHEMATICS
Pattern/sequences

What patterns can be made by joining the corners of 3/4/6/8/etc.-sided regular shapes? Use the maps created in the Geography box to devise sequencing cards.

Symmetry

Explore line and rotational symmetry by 'freezing' the movements as the children dance figures such as 'casting out' and 'stars'.

Angles

Allow the children to experiment with the language of angles when devising notation for the dance.

Number

Counting in groups of 8.

UP *the sides* & DOWN *the middle*

The Whole Curriculum

The contribution that traditional dance makes to the social, spiritual, moral and cultural development of children is invaluable.

- it promotes respect for others;
- it develops working relationships in pairs and groups;
- it encourages us to reflect upon aspects of our own and others' cultures;
- it provides opportunities to reflect on our lives and the human condition.

CULTURAL DIVERSITY

There is a great deal of healthy debate in dance education on the meaning of the term 'traditional British dances'. Ideas and opinions vary according to locality, region, political inclination, experience and knowledge.

The focus of this pack is largely on folk dances that have originated in England. It is important to remember, however, that the study of such dances is only one element of the dance programme in schools. In order to become truly dance-educated, children and young people need to gain knowledge and experience of a variety of dance forms.

All the dances presented in this pack are used as part of family or community celebrations, such as wedding receptions, P.T.A. events, harvest homes, and so on. You may like to compare them with celebratory dances from other cultures.

Chapter 2
GETTING STARTED

This chapter is designed to equip the non-specialist teacher to work with traditional folk dance. Use it with the tutorial on Side A of the cassette to make yourself feel at home with the subject, and comfortable about working in the classroom.

Characteristics of the Music

The following are the most commonly used English folk dance rhythms.

JIG
The jig is in a 6/8 time signature. It sounds bright and lively, and is fairly quick.

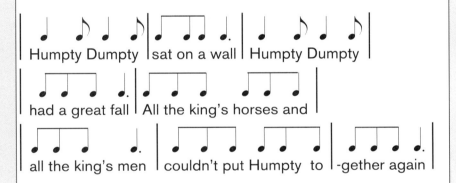

POLKA AND REEL
There is a whole family of rhythms played in 4/4 time signatures, amongst which are polkas and reels. Both these dance rhythms may sound slower than jigs, and there are normally fewer notes in each bar.

A polka has a very pronounced 1–2–3–4 rhythm, with the emphasis on the first beat.

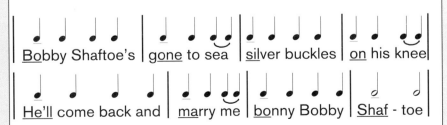

A reel sounds very similar to a polka, but is slightly 'flatter': 1–2–3–4. It doesn't have the same emphasis on the first beat.

Rhythms
Don't worry if you experience some difficulty with rhythms at first. When you come to work with the dances you will find the notations (see pages 29–46) will tell you what rhythm and length of tune is appropriate for each dance.

Humpty Dumpty sat on a wall is a jig.

Polkas and reels are more or less interchangeable, so don't worry if you find it difficult to detect the difference between the two.

Bobby Shaftoe's gone to sea is a polka.

Polly put the kettle on is a reel.

HORNPIPE

The hornpipe is also in 4/4 time, but is slower than a polka or a reel. While listening to a hornpipe, try dancing on the spot to the music. It should make you want to dance a fairly slow and pronounced step-hop, i.e. right-hop, left-hop, right-hop, left-hop. The emphasis comes on the first and third beats of each bar.

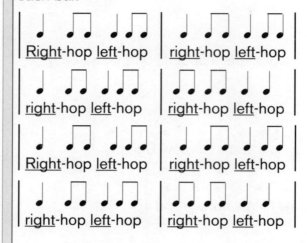

WALTZ

The waltz is in a 3/4 time signature and tends to be played at quite a steady speed.

Listen to a waltz, and try counting a slow, steady 1–2–3, 1–2–3 to the music. One count of 1–2–3 will fill one bar of music:

Notice how the first beat of each bar is stressed.

There are other rhythms in the English country dance tradition, but those described above are the most common and easily identifiable, and the ones to which children will most readily respond.

PHRASING

British folk dance tunes are usually written and played in phrases (or sections) of multiples of eight bars of music. Usually a tune will have two (or three) different 8-bar phrases, each phrase being repeated before moving on to the next, so that the music will last for 32 bars (or 48 bars) before starting again from the beginning.

It is important to be aware of the phrasing and structure of traditional dance music because the component parts of a dance follow the same pattern.

When you start working on the dance notations that follow, you will see that the figures are set against an abbreviation (A.1., etc.) for the phrasing of the music. Remember that each section consists of eight bars:

	Music	Dance
A.1.	First 8-bar phrase	First figure
A.2.	The same 8-bar phrase, repeated	Second figure
B.1.	Second 8-bar phrase	Third figure
B.2.	Repeat of the second 8-bar phrase	Fourth figure
A.1.	The music starts again from the beginning	The dance starts again

Side A of the cassette will help you understand the phrasing of the music and how it is divided into these sections of eight bars. Try to be aware of the length of each phrase of music. Listen to the way in which each musical phrase is repeated; you might wish to count the bars of music, but you may prefer not to count out loud.

When you feel confident about identifying the examples on Side A of the cassette, put your knowledge to the test by listening to some of the music on Side B.

Don't worry if you find yourself counting up to sixteen during an 8-bar phrase. People count music at different speeds, especially in something like a hornpipe. The important thing is that you hear when the phrases start and finish.

Choose a track from Side B of the cassette. Each tune is preceded by a short introduction of two bars of music (in the case of the band tracks, the introduction is played by a solo fiddle). You will then hear the first 8-bar phrase (A.1.). When you hear the same 8-bar phrase being repeated, you will know that you are moving into the second section of the dance (A.2.).

When the tune changes to a different phrase of music you will know that this is the start of the third section of the dance

Notes
Take your children through this same process. Get them to listen to the various rhythms, and then help them to hear the phrasing of the music. You might like to ask them to count the bars.

You will need to be aware that some tunes appear to start repeating themselves after four bars (e.g. in *Fred Pigeon's Polka*, bars 1–2–3 and 5–6–7 of the A phrase are the same; the only difference appears in bars 4 and 8).

UP *the sides* & DOWN *the middle*

(B.1.), and when you hear that 8-bar phrase being repeated you will know that you are entering the fourth section of the dance (B.2.). At the end of this phrase, you will have heard four phrases of eight bars each – 32 bars in all. In a 48-bar tune you will then hear the fifth and sixth sections of the dance (C.1. and C.2.).

When the music starts to play the first 8-bar phrase once more (A.1.) you will know that you are starting the dance again.

Characteristics of the Dances

The dances in this pack are English social dances. These are the sorts of dances seen at family and community celebrations. Descriptions of such events can be found in a number of books, and in particular in Thomas Hardy's writings. Hardy himself played the fiddle at local dances, as did his father and grandfather before him. The tradition continues today at such occasions as wedding receptions, barn dances, harvest suppers, and church, village or football club socials, all round the country. Folk dancing has more participants than almost any other form of social dance, and is an ideal way of building home/school links.

This form of social dancing is also referred to as 'country dancing', 'barn dancing' or simply 'folk dancing'. In recent years the term 'ceilidh dancing' (a Celtic word, pronounced kay-lee) has been used to mean the same thing.

There are several other kinds of dance in the English folk dance tradition. The main ones are:

- morris dances (ceremonial dances, mostly from the Cotswolds, Lancashire, Cheshire, the Welsh borders and the Cambridgeshire Fens);
- sword dances (from Yorkshire and the Durham coalfield area);
- solo clog dances (from Lancashire, Westmorland and County Durham);
- solo step dances and broom dances (particularly found in surviving traditions from Dartmoor and Suffolk, and among families of travellers);
- maypole dances.

SET DANCES

English social dances are 'set' dances, i.e. they consist of a sequence of movements which fit with the phrasing of the music. The first movement of the dance starts with the first phrase of the music, and every time this first phrase of music comes round, so the sequence of the dance starts again.

(It should be mentioned at this point that there are a small number of traditional English social dances which are an exception to this, in that the figures are 'unphrased', i.e. they do not fit into an exact number of bars of music, but such dances are quite rare.)

FIGURES
The social dance traditions of England, Ireland, Scotland, Wales and North America all follow this same pattern of repeating set sequences of movements. The movements in the dances are called 'figures'. Descriptions of individual figures are given with the dance notations (Chapter 5) and in the Glossary of Terms.

FORMATIONS
English social dances use a variety of formations – also sometimes referred to as 'a set' (see Glossary of Terms, page 47). See table on pages 20–21 for the most commonly used formations.

PROGRESSION
The dances also often contain a 'progression', during which couples either move to a new position in the set or change partners.

STEPS
To dance well is to respond to the rhythm of the music, both with your feet and with the rest of your body. People respond to rhythms in different ways. There is not a right or a wrong way to move your feet in English social dance.

These notes are intended purely as guidelines to some of the ways in which the dancer's feet may respond to various dance rhythms. Do not regard them as hard-and-fast rules.

Jigs are usually danced with either a skip step or a light 'walk'. If a walking step is used, try to encourage the children to give lift to their bodies, rather than just walking flatly round the room.

Polkas and reels tend to be danced either with a slower skip step or by stepping 1–2–3–hop for each bar of music.

Hornpipes are often danced with a steady step-hop, with two of these (i.e. right-hop, left-hop) to every bar of music.

Waltz: Try to help children feel the stress on the first beat (1–2–3, 1–2–3) and to step accordingly.

UP *the sides* & DOWN *the middle*

Formations

A circle dance is for any number of pairs, forming a large circle round the room:

A Sicilian circle dance is made up of a series of small circles of two pairs dancing with each other at the edge of the room. One pair faces anti-clockwise round the room, the other faces clockwise, so that the effect is of a large circle with pair facing pair all the way round its perimeter:

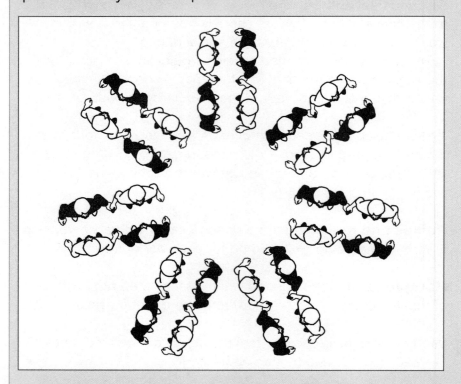

UP *the sides* & DOWN *the middle*

A couple dance is where each person dances with a partner, with any number of pairs dancing at the same time. Couples usually move anti-clockwise round the room:

A square dance is normally for four pairs, each pair forming one side of the square. The pairs tend to be numbered according to the position of the dancers in relation to the musicians, thus:

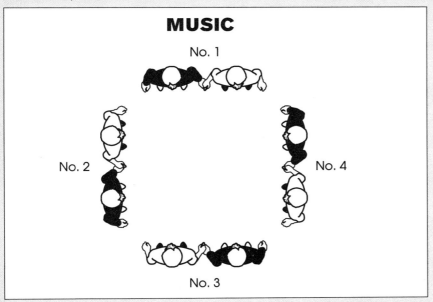

A longways dance is in a double line formation, with partners dancing on opposite sides of the set:

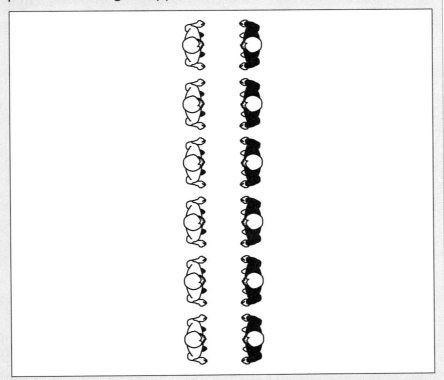

UP *the sides* & DOWN *the middle*

Partners and Gender Issues

Traditional social dances are normally danced in pairs, i.e. each person dancing with a partner, though two of the dances in this pack are danced in threes.

The dance notations have been worded so as to render it unnecessary to impose a regime of mixed-gender couples. However, you may like to think of a way of establishing who is who in each pair, since in some dance formations it is necessary to return to one's original side or place in the set. You may, for example, establish identities by using coloured bands or giving dancers labels such as 'apples' and 'bananas'.

We recommend that you consider making no reference to gender when working with your children. There is often a resistance to dance, particularly among boys, and children can be subjected to the derision of their peers if they are forced to dance in mixed-gender couples. Our experience is that it is best to let children dance with a partner of their own choice. Additionally, boys are more likely to accept social dance if they see male teachers participating in or leading the activity.

UP *the sides* & DOWN *the middle*

Chapter 3
PREPARING YOUR CHILDREN TO DANCE

The activities described in this chapter provide suitable material for warming up and for introducing and practising some of the basic skills and concepts associated with traditional dances.

Warming up

You should always start any strenuous activity with a warm-up. Use the following exercises:

- bend and straighten knees;
- bounce gently up and down without jumping;
- with weight on one foot, alternately place heel and toe of other foot on floor;
- rise up on to balls of feet, then lower; repeat with alternate feet.

Safety point
Before dance activity, ensure that ankle and knee joints are prepared by mobilising them gently.

Basic Skills

Use any of the dance tunes on Side B of the cassette for this activity. Take the children through a process of exploring different steps and movements. Use some of the following tasks to raise children's awareness of the physical and social skills that dance demands.

STEPS
Walk, jog, skip, gallop to the beat.
Keeping the same pulse, travel at different speeds.
Small steps/large steps.
On the spot/travelling.
Encourage children to make up their own steps: e.g. how many different walking steps can they find?
Steps with leg gestures, e.g. step kick.
Articulate different parts of the foot, e.g. heel and toe.
Jump with feet apart, together, crossed, etc.

SPATIAL AWARENESS
Walk, jog, skip or gallop:

- on the spot, around the room, in and out of others;
- changing direction on command/on own initiative;

- forwards, backwards, sideways;
- in straight, curved, zig-zag, figure of eight pathways.

In a circle:

- travel sideways, forwards, backwards.

PHRASING
Going and stopping/on the spot and travelling.
Respond to the phrasing of the music – counting in eights and using all of each musical phrase.
Respond to structure by changing action when the music changes: e.g. eight bars walking, eight bars stamping, eight bars skipping, eight bars clapping.

CO-ORDINATION, RHYTHM AND PATTERN
Using hands: shake, clap, tap knees/shoulders/head.
Create simple patterns: e.g. galloping sideways – eight steps left, eight right, four left, four right, two left, two right, four on the spot, then repeat whole pattern.

RELATIONSHIPS
Follow-my-leader, travelling in twos, threes, fours, whole class.
Holding hands, walk, skip and turn with a partner.
Facing a partner, travel towards/away/sideways.
Turn a partner, and turn with a partner.
Explore a variety of partner holds.
Travel alone in and out of spaces.
On a given signal make groups of two/three/four/five/six.
Further instructions could be given: e.g. in groups of five make a circle, in groups of four make a star, in groups of three make a line.

COMPOSITION SKILLS
Ask children to create their own patterns using, for example, claps, taps and stamps.
Ask them to combine a limited number of actions (alone, in twos or in small groups).
Encourage them to experiment with different movement sequences:

- on the spot – travel – on the spot;
- straight pathway – curvy pathway – circular pathway;
- travel – turn – jump;
- using three different partner holds, travel – turn – travel.

Note
Remember to emphasise eye contact!

Chapter 4
CREATING NEW FOLK DANCES

A logical step forward from Chapter 3, and once you have tried a few dances from Chapter 5, is to work with your children to create new folk dances.

Creating new folk dances in the class is an exciting, dynamic process. We have found that it is also one in which children with relatively low academic achievement levels can often shine and take the lead.

Begin by choosing the music you and the children wish to work from, and remind yourselves of the length of each musical phrase.

Then, with the children working in small groups of, say, two, four or six, ask each group to decide on one movement or figure that they would like to suggest for inclusion in the final dance. The figures they choose may be ones which they have already used in a dance, or they could be something completely new. Encourage them to devise dance figures rather than gymnastic movements.

Once the groups have decided on their figures, get each group in turn to demonstrate their work to the rest of the class. Make sure that all the class is both encouraging and positive in this process of peer evaluation.

The next step is to try to fit some of the children's ideas into a dance sequence. Remember that a 32-bar dance will need only four figures. It may well be possible to amalgamate ideas from different groups in the class so as to incorporate as many of the children's ideas as possible. Encourage the children to teach their ideas to the rest of the class, particularly by use of demonstration. Try to guide the process of assembling the dance so that, while the ideas used are those of the children, the figures of the final dance flow naturally into each other.

Throughout the process of creating a new folk dance, remember to:

- encourage innovation;
- encourage experimentation;
- ensure that what is created is a dance and not gymnastics;
- make the figures of the dance flow naturally into each other;
- ensure that the dance fits the music;
- consider the creative inspiration for the dance.

Inspiration
Take advantage of a special event which is due to take place, perhaps in your school or community, as the inspiration and impetus to create a new dance for the class or school.

You may like to consider adopting, or adapting, the 'Do–Make–View' model (see page 26).

Heva (see page 34) was created by children in Cornwall.

Notes
Encourage the children to devise their own system of dance notation, using skills gained from other areas of the curriculum (see *The Snowball* model, pages 12–13).

Once the creative process has been completed, hold a class discussion to choose a name for the new dance.

UP *the sides* & DOWN *the middle*

Dance as Art
the 'Do-Make-View' model
Unit of work for pupils in Years 4 and 5

Aim: to learn and perform a traditional British dance, *Up the Sides and Down the Middle* (see page 36), and apply knowledge, skills and understanding to the composition and evaluation of a new dance (see Dance composition, page 9).

	Do	Make	View
Tasks	Learn and perform *Up the Sides and Down the Middle*.	In small groups compose a dance to interpret the title.	Notate own dance and compare with the original.
Programme of Study (Key Stage 2)	Control movements. Vary direction. Sustain energetic activity.	Respond to music. Compose movements.	
End of Key Stage Description (Key Stage 2)	Practise, improve and refine performance. Repeat series of movements previously performed.	Find solutions. Respond imaginatively to challenges. Work as a member of a team.	Make simple judgements.
Additionally	Show poise and co-ordination. Use appropriate qualities. Use space accurately.	Explore and express ideas. Select appropriate movements. Contribute to discussion on structure. Use simple compositional devices, e.g. repetition and variation.	Look perceptively at dance movements. Describe and compare dances. Appreciate musical form and structure.

Chapter 5
THE DANCES

The dances described in this chapter have been chosen and placed in appropriate sequence to give a progression in terms of both skills learned and complexity.

Page	Name of dance	New elements introduced
29	*Dorset Ring Dance*	Polka rhythm, circle dance, promenade, swing
30	*The Islington Shuffle*	Jig rhythm, back to back, balance
31	*The Cumberland Reel*	Longways dance, star, gallop, cast out
32	*The Bridge of Athlone*	Forward and back, dance through arches
33	*Buttered Peas*	Sicilian circle dance, shake hands
34	*Heva*	Processional dance, butterfly hold, dance backwards
35	*The Snowball*	Right- and left-hand turn
36	*Up the Sides and Down the Middle*	Walking step at half speed
37	*The Albert Quadrille*	Square dance, changing places in the set
38	*The Caerphilly March*	Couple dance, right- and left-arm swing
39	*The Barley Reel*	Strip the willow
40	*Three Handed Reel*	Threesome dance, cross foot stepping, reel of three
41	*Three Meet*	Basket of three
42	*Goathland Square Eight*	Cross over in couples, grand chain
43	*Soldier's Joy*	Hornpipe rhythm
44	*Steam-Boat*	Progression in a longways dance
45	*Circle Waltz*	Waltz rhythm, chassay
46	*Bonny Breast Knot*	Arm right and left with the rest of the set, change shape of set during dance

Photo: Simon Chapman

UP *the sides* & DOWN *the middle*

Dance figures
When a dance figure appears for the first time it is introduced in some detail. Thereafter it is referred to only by its name. (To locate where it is described in detail, see Glossary of Terms, page 47.)

Notes
Remember that each of the tracks on Side B of the cassette contains a short 2-bar introduction. In the case of the band tracks, this is played by a solo fiddle. The dancing should start at the end of the introduction.

There is sufficient pause between tracks to enable you to turn off your cassette player between dances.

Using the Dance Notations

The references A.1., A.2., etc. are used to help you fit the dance figures to the phrasing of the music (see Phrasing, page 17).

You will need to start by teaching the children the figures and flow of a dance. Get them to 'walk through' the figures without music so that they become familiar with the directions in which they will be moving and the figures they will be dancing.

Make them familiar with the names of the figures, so that they know exactly how to respond, for example, when they hear the words 'right-hand star'. While they are dancing with the music, you won't have much time – or much voice! – for a lengthy explanation of each figure.

CALLING

Listen to the 'calling' with the two tunes at the end of the tutorial on Side A of the cassette and notice how the call comes just before the start of each figure. Calling like this, just 'in front' of the music, will enable children to move confidently into each part of the dance at the appropriate point in the music.

Try not to call all the way through a dance. Test and help to increase the children's music/dance awareness and memory by stopping calling after, say, the third time through a dance, but be ready, of course, to give them a reminder should they need it.

MUSIC

If you travel around the country you will find that the same dances are danced to a variety of tunes. There is no 'right' tune for any of the dances in the pack, but the rhythm for any one dance will always be the same. There is sufficient variety of rhythm and length of music on Side B of the cassette to enable you to tackle all the dances in the pack, and many more besides.

For example, if you wish to dance the *Dorset Ring Dance*, you will see that the music required is a 32-bar polka. This means that the dance can be accompanied by any of the 32-bar polkas on the cassette, or any other 32-bar polka tune.

DORSET RING DANCE

(A traditional dance, collected in Burton Bradstock, Dorset)

MUSIC: 32-bar polka

FORMATION: a large circle, made up of any number of couples

A.1. Circle to the left.

A.2. Circle to the right.

B.1. Promenade ★ round the room in an anti-clockwise direction.

B.2. Keep holding hands with your partner and swing ★★ on the spot.

A.1. Start the dance again.

VARIATION: *for older children. Replace B.2. above with:*

B.2. Polka ★★★ round the edge of the room with your partner.

Dance note
Remember that the music is a polka: try to step in time with the music, don't just walk.

Dance figures
★ *PROMENADE*
Stand side by side with your partner in a cross-hand hold (right hand in right hand, left in left) and dance forwards together; don't turn round or go backwards.

★★ *SWING*
Take both hands with your partner (you could also be in a 'ballroom' hold) and pivot together on the spot in a clockwise direction.

★★★ *POLKA*
Either in a ballroom hold or by taking both hands in a cross-hand hold, dance with your partner – with a 1-2-3-hop or a step-hop – anti-clockwise round the room while turning clockwise as a couple.

History note
The dance was collected in rural Dorset. It would have been danced earlier this century, and in the last century, by ordinary working men and women. The polka rhythm is now regarded as part of the English country-dance tradition, but it was introduced into this country in the nineteenth century.

UP *the sides* & DOWN *the middle*

Dance figures

★ **BACK TO BACK**

Face your partner and move forward, passing each other by the right shoulder (see diagram). Then move across to the right, passing back to back (see shaded figures in diagram). Come backwards to your original place. (This figure is sometimes called a 'Do-si-do'.)

★★ **BALANCE**

Step and hop on one foot, while you kick the other foot across in front of you. Do this on alternate feet (left and kick, right and kick, left and kick, right and kick).

THE ISLINGTON SHUFFLE

(A new dance devised by Francis Shergold, a member of a traditional morris-dancing family from Bampton, Oxfordshire)

MUSIC: 32-bar jig

FORMATION: A circle, made up of any number of couples

A.1. Bars 1–4   Join hands round the circle and dance into the middle (four steps) and out again (four steps).

Bars 5–8   Do the same again.

A.2. Bars 1–4   Face your partner and dance a back to back ★ passing by the right shoulder.

Bars 5–8   Do the same again, but pass by the left shoulder.

B.1. Bars 1–4   Balance (step and kick) ★★ with your partner four times.

Bars 5–8   Take both hands with your partner and swing.

B.2. Keep holding hands and promenade round the room in an anti-clockwise direction.

A.1. Start the dance again.

VARIATION: *for older children. Replace A.2. above with:*

A.2. First back to back as above, but in Bars 5-8 turn round to face your neighbour (the person on the other side of you in the circle) and dance a back to back with them. You are changing partners. Stay with this person until the next time you do back to backs, when you change partners once again.

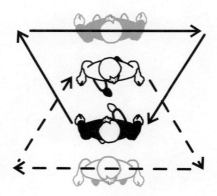

UP *the sides* & DOWN *the middle*

THE CUMBERLAND REEL

(A traditional dance from the Lake District)

MUSIC: 32-bar jig

FORMATION: a longways dance for four couples

A.1. Bars 1–4 Top two couples dance a right-hand star ★, while the bottom two couples do the same.

Bars 5–8 Left-hand stars.

A.2. Bars 1–4 Top couple take both hands with your partner and gallop ★★ down the middle of the set.

Bars 5–8 The same couple gallop to the top again.

B.1. Top couple let go hands, separate, and cast out from the top of the set (one person turns left, the other right). The rest follow them to the bottom of the set. The leading couple make an arch at the bottom and stay there; everyone else, meet your partner at the bottom and dance through the arch and up the middle.

B.2. The new top couple face the top, take both hands in a cross-hand hold, and lead all the other couples in a promenade to the left, all the way round to the bottom of the set and then up to the top again.

A.1. Start the dance again. Everyone will now be in a new position in the set.

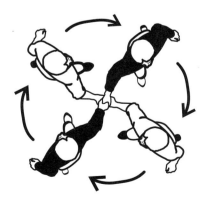

Dance figures

★ *STAR*
In your groups of two couples, hold right hands across in a star shape and move round clockwise (see diagram). Then let go your hands, turn round and come back the other way, making a star shape with your left hands.

★★ *GALLOP*
A lively sideways movement with a bounding step (feet moving apart, close, apart, close, etc.), danced while facing your partner. Usually partners hold both hands with each other.

UP *the sides* & DOWN *the middle*

THE BRIDGE OF ATHLONE

(An American version of a traditional Irish dance)

MUSIC: 48-bar jig

FORMATION: a longways set for five couples

A.1. Join hands along your own side of the set. The two lines dance forward to meet, back again, then forward and cross over to the other side (one line make arches while you do this, and the other side let go hands to go under the arches).

A.2. Do the same again, but the other line make the arches this time.

B.1. Top couple gallop down the middle of the set and back again.

B.2. Top couple cast out to the bottom of the set and make an arch, while everyone else follows, coming through the arch with your partner. (See *The Cumberland Reel*, page 31).

C.1. The top four couples all make a two-handed arch with your partner, while the bottom couple move up the set and back again – one person dancing up the set under the arches and back down the outside, while their partner dances up the outside and then down through the arches.

C.2. All swing with your partner.

A.1. Start the dance again. (Remember that there is a new couple at the top.)

BUTTERED PEAS

(A traditional dance from the Yorkshire Dales)

MUSIC: 32-bar polka

FORMATION: Sicilian circle (see page 20)

A.1. Take hands in a circle of four and dance to the left (four bars) then to the right (four bars).

A.2. Right-hand star and left-hand star.

B.1. Bars 1–4   Shake hands and clap with your neighbour (i.e. the person who is next to you and who is not your partner):

shake right, right, right; clap your own hands together three times;
shake left, left, left; clap, clap, clap.

Bars 5–8   Swing that person.

B.2. Do the same as in B.1., but this time with your partner.

A.1. Start the dance again.

VARIATION: *for older children. Replace B.2. above with:*

B.2. *While you swing, move past the pair with whom you have been dancing and move on in order to start the dance again in the next A.1. phrase with a new couple.*

UP *the sides* & DOWN *the middle*

HEVA

*(A processional dance devised in 1961 by children at Crantock Street School, Newquay, Cornwall, with their teacher, Miss Rowland. The dance appears in **Corollyn**, see Other Sources, page 48.)*

MUSIC: 16- or 32-bar polka

FORMATION: a procession of pairs of couples, one couple behind the other. The dance can also be done in a circle, with each pair facing anti-clockwise round the room.

A. Bars 1–4 In a butterfly hold ★ promenade forward, stepping slightly out to the right on the first bar, to the left on the next, to the right on the next, and on the fourth turn round to face the other way (without letting go with your hands and without changing position, you both turn on the spot and to the right).

Bars 5–8 Continue to dance in the same direction round the room. This means that, as you have turned round, you will now be dancing backwards.

B. Bars 1–4 Let go of your partner and face the couple next to you (one couple will have to turn round to face the other couple), then dance into the middle of your group of four (1–2–3–clap), then out again (1–2–3–4), then in (1–2–3–clap) and out again (1–2–3–4).

Bars 5–8 Take your partner in a cross-hand hold and swing.

A. Without letting go your partner's hands, face your original direction and start again.

Dance figure
★ *BUTTERFLY HOLD*
Stand side by side with your partner. The person on the left put your right arm across your partner's shoulders to hold right hands above their right shoulder, and hold left hands in front of you at waist level.

UP *the sides* & DOWN *the middle*

THE SNOWBALL

(An adaptation of a new dance devised by Anne Welch of Biggin Hill, Kent)

MUSIC: 48-bar jig

FORMATION: a longways dance for five couples. (The couple in the top position is the first couple, the next is the second, and so on.)

A.1. Bars 1–4   First couple right-hand turn ★ with your partner.

Bars 5–8   First couple left-hand turn with your partner.

A.2. First and second couple dance a right- and left-hand star.

B.1. First, second and third couples join hands together and circle left and right.

B.2. First, second, third and fourth couples all dance a back to back with your partner (twice).

C.1. Fifth couple gallop up the middle of the set and then back again.

C.2. Fifth couple face down the set and cast out from the bottom. Everyone else follow on your own side of the set. Fifth couple make an arch when you get to the top, while everyone else meet your partner above the arch, dance through the arch and down the middle. Swing your partner if you have time.

A.1. Start the dance again. (Note that everyone has now changed position in the set: the couple that was at the bottom is now the first couple, and everyone else has moved one place down the set.)

Dance figure
★ *RIGHT- OR LEFT-HAND TURN*
Hold right hands with your partner at just below shoulder height and move clockwise to turn all the way round, finishing in your original position.
Move anti-clockwise with a left-hand turn.

UP THE SIDES AND DOWN THE MIDDLE

(A traditional dance collected from Mrs Nora Clayton of Upwey, Dorset)

MUSIC: 32-bar jig

FORMATION: longways dance for four or five couples. (The couple standing at the top of the set is the first couple.)

A.1. Bars 1–4 Join hands along your own side of the set and all balance four times.

   Bars 5–8 Lines cross over to the other side, one line making arches, the other letting go their hands as they cross and going under the arches.

A.2. Do the same again, but the other line makes the arches.

B.1. Up the sides and down the middle:

   First couple walk slowly down the middle of the set, while holding one hand in the air with your partner to make an arch.

   Everyone else face up the set and follow the second couple, who separate and cast out to the bottom, meet your partner and come up the middle again under the first couple's arch.

B.2. All swing your partner.

A.1. Start the dance again. (Remember that there is now a new first couple.)

THE ALBERT QUADRILLE

(A dance from Dorset; notes about the dance were found by Dave Townsend of Witney, Oxfordshire, in manuscripts in the Bodleian Library, Oxford)

MUSIC: 48-bar polka

FORMATION: a square set of four couples. (Head couples are the couples in positions 1 and 3, the side couples are those in positions 2 and 4. We have referred to the person on the left in each couple as X, and the person on the right as Y.)

A.1. Bars 1–4 Head couples take hands and dance forward (four steps) and back (four steps), then

Bars 5–8 let go hands and dance a back to back with the person you are facing.

A.2. Side couples do the same.

B.1. Bars 1–4 Head couples join hands in the centre of the set and circle left half-way round, so that you have changed sides, then step back into the other couple's place.

Bars 5–6 The two Xs cross to return to their original place.

Bars 7–8 The two Ys do the same.

B.2. Side couples do the same.

C.1. All make a right- and left-hand star: put your arm round your partner's waist, and the Ys make the right-hand star. When you make the left-hand star, Ys let go with your right hands (but keep your arm round your partner) and turn round with your partner so that the Xs make the left-hand star.

C.2. Stay in this position, standing side by side with your partner, take both hands and balance four times, then promenade three places round the set.

A.1. Start the dance again, but remember that you are now in a new position in the set.

Dance note
PROGRESSION
The promenade will have made you change position in the set (i.e. you will have 'progressed'), so if you were a head couple, you will now be in a side couple position, and if you were in a side couple position, you will now be a head couple.

History note
THE VICTORIANS
The Dorset Ring Dance, Up the Sides and Down the Middle, and *The Albert Quadrille* were noted down in Dorset earlier this century. The people who were dancing them when they were 'collected' would have represented a direct link with the Victorian era, and the dances would almost certainly have been danced during the Victorian period.

The Quadrille was a popular dance form with the Victorians and the name of this dance refers to Albert, the Prince Consort.

Many of the other dances in this pack have similar regional origins and would have been danced in the Victorian period, e.g. *Buttered Peas* in the Yorkshire Dales and The *Cumberland Reel* in the Lake District.

THE CAERPHILLY MARCH

(A traditional Welsh dance)

MUSIC: 32-bar polka

FORMATION: a couple dance

A.1. Stand side by side with your partner, holding nearest hand, and

- Bars 1–4 step away from each other, together again, and dance forward for three steps, then let go and both turn round on the fourth step;
- Bars 5–8 step away from each other, together again, and dance forward for four steps to your original place.

A.2. Bars 1–4 Link right arms, and dance a right-arm swing.

Bars 5–8 Left-arm swing.

B.1. Bars 1–4 Clap with your partner: your own hands together, right hands with your partner, your own hands together, left with your partner, together, across on your own chest, both hands with your partner.

Bars 5–8 Do the same clapping again.

B.2. Swing your partner, while dancing round the room.

A.1. Start the dance again.

VARIATION: *The Double Gloucester March*
(Devised by Dave Hunt of Telford, Shropshire)

Replace A.1. and B.1. above with:

A.1. Bars 1–4 *In a butterfly hold, dance forward for two bars, turn (without letting go your hands or crossing with your partner) then backwards for two bars.*

Bars 5–8 *The same again to return to your original place.*

B.1. Bars 1–4 *Clap with your partner: your own hands together, right hands with your partner, together, left hands, together, under your right leg, together, under your left leg.*

Bars 5–8 *Do the same clapping again.*

Dance note
When linking right arms, support each other by 'giving weight' (i.e. using the tension in your arms to support your partner). By doing this you make a counterbalance with your partner to help you swing better. This is a good introduction to the 'Strip the Willow' figure in *The Barley Reel*, see page 39.

THE BARLEY REEL

(A traditional dance of Scottish origin, also called The Barley Brae)

MUSIC: 48-bar jig

FORMATION: longways dance for four couples. (Call the people on one side of the set X, and those on the other side Y.)

A.1. Join hands along your own side of the set, dance forward (four steps) and back (four steps), then forward again and cross over to the other side of the set (one line make arches, the other line let go as they go underneath the arches.)

A.2. Do the same again, but the other line make the arches.

B.1. and B.2. First couple strip the willow ★ down the set until they reach the bottom. They stay at the bottom and make an arch.

C.1. Second couple separate to cast out and lead everyone else down the outside of the set. Meet your partner at the bottom and come up the middle through the first couple's arch.

C.2. All swing your partner.

A.1. Start the dance again. Remember that there is now a new first couple.

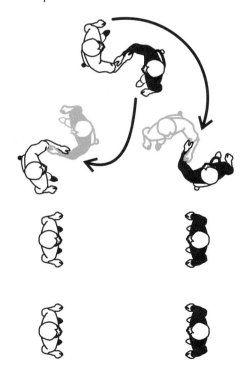

UP *the sides* & DOWN *the middle*

Dance figure

★ STRIP THE WILLOW

First couple link right arms and turn half-way (or one-and-a-half times) so that you change sides (see diagram). Letting go with your right arms, link left arms with the next person on the other side (see shaded figures in diagram). Turn with them so that you are facing your partner again in the middle of the set. Let go with your left arm, and first couple turn once round with the right arm. Then link left arms with the next person down on the other side of the set, and so on until the first couple reach the bottom.

Dance note

In the strip the willow figure, if you are the couple which is moving down the set, you always give right arm to your partner before giving left to the next person down on the other side of the set.

If you are not part of the leading couple, you move only once – when one of the leading couple links left arms with you – then stay in your place to be ready for the cast out in C.1.

THREE HANDED REEL

(A traditional dance from Sidbury, Devon)

MUSIC: 32-bar jig

FORMATION: lines of three round the whole room, radiating from the centre of the room. The 'insides' are those towards the centre of the room, the 'middles' are in the centre of the threesome, and the 'outsides' are those towards the outside of the room.

A.1. Middles face outsides and both step for eight bars (feet cross and apart eight times, alternate feet in front).

A.2. Middles do the same with the insides.

B.1. Bars 1–4 Middles link right arms with the insides and swing.

Bars 5–8 Middles link left arms with the outsides and swing.

B.2. Middles face the insides and all three dance a reel of three ★.

A.1. Start the dance again. (At the end of the reel of three, the middles could move one place anti-clockwise round the room to start the dance again with the next two people.)

Dance figure

★ REEL OF THREE

Think of a reel of three as dancing a figure of eight with all three dancers moving at the same time.

Inside person (diagram A): face the middle person and pass right shoulders with them. Pass left shoulders with the next and turn left as you reach the outside person's position. Pass left and then right shoulders again and return to your original position.

Middle person (diagram B): face the inside person, pass right shoulders with them, and turn right as you reach their position. Pass right shoulders with the person who is now coming towards you, pass left shoulders and turn left, and pass left shoulders again with the next to return to your original position.

Outside person (diagram C): pass left shoulders and move between the other two dancers, passing right shoulders with the next. As you reach the inside person's place, turn right. Pass right then left shoulders and return to your original position.

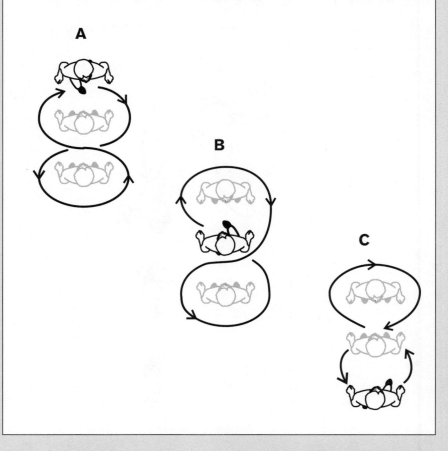

40

UP *the sides* & DOWN *the middle*

THREE MEET

(A traditional dance from Gloucestershire)

MUSIC: 32-bar jig

FORMATION: lines of three round the edge of the room, each line facing another line and all radiating from the centre of the room

A.1. Link arms in your lines of three and dance forward to meet the threesome you are facing, then back again, and then forward, passing to the right of them. Turn as a line (still with your arms linked) to face your original position (you will have changed places with the other threesome, but still be facing them).

A.2. Do all that again so that you return to your original position.

B.1. All six of you join hands and circle left and right.

B.2. Now in your threes, make a basket of three ★ and dance round to the left; as you do so, change places with the other threesome.

A.1. Start the dance again, facing the same direction as when you started the dance: you will now be facing a new line of three.

Dance figure
★ *BASKET OF THREE*
Cross your hands and hold hands with each other in a circle. Use the tension in your arms and elbows in order to 'give weight' so that the members of your threesome act as a counterbalance for each other. All use your right foot as a pivot and move round to the left.

UP *the sides* & DOWN *the middle*

GOATHLAND SQUARE EIGHT

(A traditional dance from the North Yorkshire Moors)

MUSIC: 32-bar polka

FORMATION: a square set of four couples

A.1. Join hands round the set and circle left and right.

A.2. All take inside hand with your partner and:

Bars 1–2   first couple cross over and change places with third couple (first couple making an arch);

Bars 3–4   second couple cross over and change places with fourth couple (second couple arch);

Bars 5–6   third couple cross over and change places with first couple (third couple arch);

Bars 7–8   fourth couple cross over and change places with second couple (fourth couple arch).

This will bring everyone back to their original position in the set.

B.1. Face your partner and dance a grand chain ★ round the set. When you meet your partner (half-way round the set) swing your partner.

B.2. As in B.1. continuing to your original place.

A.1. Start the dance again.

Dance note
There is not much time to complete the moves in A.2. in the allotted eight bars of music, so you need to be alert.

Dance figure
★ GRAND CHAIN
Face your partner and move round the set by passing right hands with your partner (see diagram), left with the next person, right with the next, left with the next, etc. Keep moving in the same direction: don't turn round!

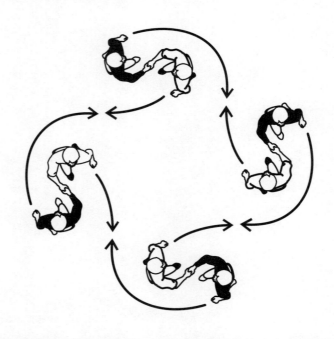

UP **the sides** & DOWN **the middle**

SOLDIER'S JOY

(A traditional dance collected by Cecil Sharp at Blue Anchor, Somerset)

MUSIC: 32-bar hornpipe

FORMATION: longways dance for three couples

A.1. All take both hands with your partner in a cross-hand hold, face the top of the set, and promenade all the way round to the left, finishing where you started from.

A.2. Bars 1–4 Facing your partner, step back, then move forward to meet, and turn on the spot all the way round to the right (finish facing your partner again).

Bars 5–8 Take both hands with your partner in a fairly wide, uncrossed hold and circle all the way round to your left.

B.1. First couple face down the set, taking inside hands, and dance down the middle of the set, then let go hands, turn and dance back up again.

B.2. While you all swing ★ with your partner, first and second couples change places with each other.

A.1. Start the dance again, but be aware that the first couple is now in the middle of the set (see Dance note). Everything will be the same as before, except:

B.1. Middle (i.e. first) couple dance down the middle and come back to their middle position, and

B.2. Everyone swing and middle and bottom couples change places.

Dance notes

The music for this dance is a hornpipe. Remember to get your children to step to the music, not to walk!

Remember that you are a first couple for twice through the dance – once in the top position, then once in the middle position. The third time through the dance, the couple which is then in the top position becomes the new first couple, and the fifth time through the dance, the couple then in the top position becomes the first couple.

Dance figure
★ SWING IN A HORNPIPE RHYTHM
Face your partner and hold hands in a cross-hand hold, bending your elbows so that your hands are at about chest height. Swing with a step-hop, pivoting round to your left.

History note
Cecil Sharp, who noted down this dance while visiting Blue Anchor in Somerset, was one of the foremost collectors of traditional dances, tunes and songs in the late-nineteenth and early-twentieth centuries. He had to do all his 'collecting' by hand. He started collecting folk songs almost exactly sixty years before the audio cassette was invented, so dance movements and words of songs were written out in longhand, and tunes were also noted down manually.

STEAM-BOAT

(A traditional dance from Devon)

MUSIC: 32-bar hornpipe

FORMATION: longways dance for any number of couples. (Each couple is either a first couple or a second couple: the couple nearest the top is a first, the next is a second, the next is a first, and so on.)

A.1. Bars 1–4   All the first couples face down the middle and step forward. As you pass between your second couple, link arms with them and all carry on stepping down the room in a line of four abreast.

Bars 4–8   Let go with your arms, turn round on the spot, link arms and all dance up the set again to return to your original position.

A.2. Bars 1–4   First couples dance down the middle of the set, followed by their second couple.

Bars 5–8   All turn round on the spot, and second couple make an arch with your partner. First couple dance through the arch and second couple follow them back up the set so that you all return to your original positions.

B.1. Dance a right- and left-hand star with the same couple.

B.2. Take a cross-hand hold with your partner and swing.

A.1. Start the dance again.

Dance note

In B.2. it is traditional for the two couples to change places as they swing – the first couples moving one place down the set, the second couples moving one place up the set. You then start the dance again with a new couple.

When this happens, the couples which have just reached either end of the set will not have another couple to dance with. They take a rest for once through the dance, and when they rejoin the dance next time through, they will have changed number: i.e. the couple which rested at the top of the set will rejoin as a first couple, and the couple which rested at the bottom of the set will rejoin as a second couple.

CIRCLE WALTZ

(A traditional dance, as danced in the border villages of Northumberland)

MUSIC: 32-bar waltz

FORMATION: a circle made up of any number of couples. (The person on the left in each couple is called X, the person on the right is called Y.)

A.1. Bars 1–2   Join hands round the circle and all sway forward and back (moving your arms as well as your feet).

      Bars 3–4   All the Ys turn away from your partner, moving to the other side of the person on your right.

      Bars 5–8   Do all that again.

A.2. Repeat all the above: you will all finish a long way from your original partner.

B.1. Take nearest hands with this new partner and sway with your inside hands and shoulders in towards the middle of the room, then back again, then forward again and turn half-way round (let go your hands) so that you are then facing the outside of the room. Sway forward and back and forward and turn round again, and finish facing this new partner.

B.2. In a ballroom hold, chassay ★ two slow steps towards the centre of the room, chassay two steps out again, then waltz for four bars and reform the circle.

A.1. Start the dance again.

Dance note
At the end of A.2., if you are an X, your new partner is the person on your right. If you are a Y, your new partner is the person on your left.

Dance figure
★ *CHASSAY*
A sideways movement with your partner, sliding your feet apart then closing them – either in a ballroom hold or taking both hands.

UP *the sides* & DOWN *the middle*

Dance figure
★ **ARM RIGHT AND LEFT WITH THE REST OF THE SET**
The couple in the middle of the set is the working couple. They are facing their partner, with their first corner diagonally across to their right and their second corner diagonally across to their left.

Middle couple link right arms. Turn each other to change places and move towards your first corner (see diagram A).

Give left arm to your first corner. Turn this person all the way and return to the centre of the set (see diagram B).

Repeat both moves, but give left arm to your second corner.

Turn your partner with the right again to get back to your position in the middle of the set. Everyone else stay where you are once you have been turned.

History note
Before the days of the welfare state, many villages had their own Friendly Societies to which people would subscribe as a form of insurance in case of sickness or death. One day a year these 'clubs' had a special Club Day when members processed round the village, visiting notable houses and the church, and ended the day with a feast. Club members wore a rosette or 'breast knot' as a symbol of their membership. The custom still survives in a few villages in England.

BONNY BREAST KNOT
(A traditional dance collected in Stockland, Devon, and in Somerset)

MUSIC: 32-bar polka

FORMATION: a longways dance for three couples. (People on one side of the set are the Xs, those on the other are the Ys.)

A.1. First couple lead through the second and third Ys, and cast away from each other, each passing round a Y, to come in from the top or the bottom of the set. Meet in the middle, and then lead between the second and third Xs and cast away from each other, each passing round an X.

The first X finishes at the bottom of the set between the third couple (the three of them face up the set and hold hands in a line). The first Y finishes at the top of the set between the second couple (the three of them face down the set and hold hands in a line).

A.2. Balance four times, then the first couple move to the middle place on their original sides of the set. All take hands in a line and face across the set and all balance four times again.

B.1. First couple arm right and left with the rest of the set ★.

B.2. First couple dance to the bottom of the set, and all swing your partner.

A.1. Start the dance again.

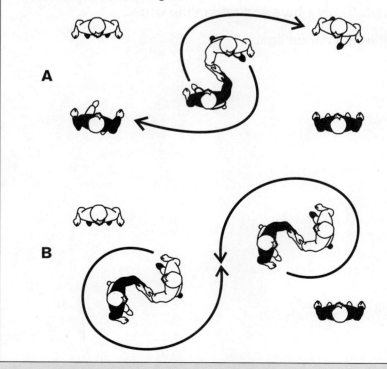

UP *the sides* & DOWN *the middle*

GLOSSARY OF TERMS

Back to back See *Islington Shuffle*, page 30. Also called 'Do-si-do'.
Balance See *Islington Shuffle*, page 30. When you 'balance and swing' you normally balance four times before you swing. Balancing in waltz time is more of a swaying movement, see *Circle Waltz*, page 45.
Basket Form a circle (the person on the left of each couple puts their arms round their neighbours' waists, while the other person in each couple puts their hands on their neighbours' shoulders), then lean slightly backwards and pivot on your right foot and move round to the left – don't go back to the right again. A basket is normally danced by a group of four people.
Note: This is the standard basket. The 'basket of three' in *Three Meet* (page 41) is an unusual figure.
Bottom The end of the set farthest from the music.
Butterfly hold See *Heva*, page 34.
Caller The person who 'teaches' the dance to those taking part, before the music starts, and who then reminds them of the figures by calling out each figure just before the appropriate point in the music.
Cast out Face up (or, occasionally, down) the set and follow your leader to turn away from the other line and towards the bottom (or top) of the set.
Chassay See *Circle Waltz*, page 45.
Cross-hand hold Hold hands with your partner, right in right, left in left. The right hands will be above the left hands.
Dip and dive A form of perpetual motion, in which each couple takes one hand with their partner and moves through the set, alternately passing under one couple's joined hands then making an arch and passing over the next. The dip and dive starts from the bottom of the set, with the bottom couple facing up the set and the other couples facing down. Each couple joins in as the leading couple meets them. Leading couple (at the bottom of the set) pass underneath the arch made by the couple facing you, then over the next couple, and so on. You will reach either end by passing over the couple coming towards you, then turn and follow them, going under the next couple coming towards you. Finish the dip and dive when you have returned to your starting position. (Those who get there first may 'fill up' the music by swinging.)
Do-si-do See 'Back to back'.
Down If you dance 'down' the set, you dance towards the bottom.
Figure of eight The same as a 'Reel of three', see *Three Handed Reel*, page 40.
First couple In a square set or longways dance, this is the couple at the top of the set. In a longways set for as many as will (see *Steam-Boat*, page 44), alternate couples down the set are each called a first couple, starting with the top couple.
Gallop See *Cumberland Reel*, page 31.
Grand chain See *Goathland Square Eight*, page 42.
Head couples In a square set, the couples in the top and bottom position (i.e. numbers 1 and 3). See page 21.
Hornpipe See page 16.
Inside hands The nearest hand to your partner.
Jig See page 15.
Ladies' chain See Square chain.
Longways set or dance See Formations, page 21.
Polka See page 15. Also a dance step, see *Dorset Ring Dance*, page 29.
Progression Couples change places during a dance so that each time they start the dance they are in a new position in the set.
Promenade See *Dorset Ring Dance*, page 29.
Promenade hold Stand side by side with your partner, holding hands with each other across and in front of you: right in right, left in left.
Rant A dance rhythm in 4/4 time, similar to a polka.
Reel See page 15. Also a weaving figure in which dancers move round each other, passing right shoulders then left, etc. A reel of three is danced by three people who weave in and out of each other in a figure of eight; see *Three Handed Reel*, page 40.
  In addition – just to make things totally confusing – the word 'reel' often appears in the name of a dance (e.g. *Cumberland Reel, Barley Reel*) even though neither a reel rhythm nor a reel figure features in the dance!
Schottische A dance rhythm in 4/4 time, rather like a 'flat' hornpipe. (Pronounced 'Shot-eesh'.)
Second couples In a longways set for as many as will, alternate couples down the length of the set are called second couples, starting with the couple next to the top; see *Steam-Boat*, page 44.
Set A small sideways stepping movement. There is a small preparatory lift of the body, then the feet move: right-left-right, lift, left-right-left, etc. This can sometimes take the place of a balance.
  Also the general term used for the group of people dancing together in whatever formation is required, e.g. square set, longways set.

Set dance See page 18.
Sicilian circle See Formations, page 20.
Side couples In a square set, the couples at the sides of the set (numbers 2 and 4). See page 21.
Square chain Danced with couple facing couple. Those on the right in each couple give right hand to each other and change places. Give left to your new partner, and as you meet them they put their right hand behind your back to turn round with you to face the other couple again. Do the same again to return to your original partner. This figure is also called a Ladies' chain.
Square set or dance See Formations, page 21.
Star See *Cumberland Reel*, page 31.
Strip the willow See *Barley Reel*, page 39.
Swing Danced by two people, either in a cross-hand or ballroom hold (we recommend the cross-hand hold when working with children). The dancers pivot round clockwise, on the right foot. For swinging in a hornpipe rhythm, see *Soldier's Joy*, page 43. It is not normal to swing in a waltz rhythm, because the music tends to be too slow.
Top The end of the set nearest the music.
Two-hand turn Take both hands with your partner and turn all the way round.
Up If you dance 'up' the set, you dance towards the top.

RESOURCES

Other traditional folk dance resources for teachers

The Community Dance Manuals are the most useful source of notations of traditional dances. They are published individually or in one volume. Available by mail order from:
The Folk Shop, Cecil Sharp House, 2 Regent's Park Road, London, NW1 7AY (Tel. 0171 284 0534)

The Folk Shop also stocks other books and recordings designed for use in schools. Check their current catalogue. Specialist books currently available include:
New Dances from Newcastle – Twelve dances devised by primary children in Newcastle upon Tyne.
Maypole Dancing – Instructions, diagrams and music (booklet and cassette).
Eight Morris Dances of England – Simple morris dances and a sword dance from Flamborough.
Scottish Country Dances for Children (book and cassette).

Other sources

Corollyn – A collection of dances, tunes and songs from Cornwall (booklet, cassette and video). Available from:
Cam Kernewek,
Meneghyjy,
Withiel, Bodmin,
Cornwall PL30 5NN

Midwinter; *Plough Monday to Hocktide*; *May* – A series of education project packs, each of which contains cross-curricular activities, folk fact sheets, songs, plays and some morris, maypole and country dances. The resource packs are linked to the seasons of the year.
Available from:
Education Dept, English Folk Dance and Song Society,
Cecil Sharp House,
2 Regent's Park Road,
London NW1 7AY
(Tel. 0171 485 2206) or from The Folk Shop (see above).

TEACHER TRAINING COURSE

Folk South West offers a one-day teacher training course to accompany this pack in association with education advisers and others in the South West (Cornwall, Devon, Dorset, Somerset and Gloucestershire).

The day is based on the contents of *Up the Sides and Down the Middle*, and is largely activity-based. It focuses on:
- developing a range of teaching strategies;
- progression and continuity;
- the process of performing, creating and appreciating;
- links with National Curriculum Dance, Music and other curriculum areas.

If you are interested in participating in or organising a training day for teachers in your area contact:
Folk South West The Stables Montacute House Montacute Somerset TA15 6XP   Tel. 01935 822911